BRING YOUR NIGHTS
WITH YOU

SAINT JULIAN PRESS

POETRY

Praise for BRING YOUR NIGHTS WITH YOU: New & Selected Poems, 1975-2015

IT IS as if all of human experience, knowledge, and geography are encoded and distilled within this new double volume of poetry by Thomas Simmons, such is the tremendous conceptual, intellectual, and sonorous range of the work. The poet incorporates so much worldly perception and literature within these pages that it is as if the reader is being offered a vision of both human and unearthly existence at once.

The drama of voice and also of diction magnify and amplify this literary magnificence, the mature work of a humanist whose learning and poetic ability extends beyond any specific personal moment, engaging with a thoroughly extensive mortal terrain. However, there exists an unseen sub-textual performative quality inside all of these poems which raises the words and lines off the page—within the mind of the reader—and which supply the language with an enigmatic non-verbal quality: simultaneous, immediate, and so profoundly finite. This uncanny *pneuma* is intrinsic to the worth of these two fine books.

It is as if the poet is foretelling his own life, but in paradoxical retrospect, such is the vivacious and vital nature of consciousness at work in these lines. It is a distinction of writing and awareness, of both sadness and fascination, as the poet's attention careers away from a *world before grace* towards an imperishable and indelible comprehension.

The poet says, *Among those I loved you were the first ... whose only choice was to prevent my ever reaching you;* and then later, *How to say good-bye when one has already gone?* Such sentiments are the mysterious and contrary threads that run through the fabric of this wonderful poetry binding the emotions and material detail into one strong medium, a tissue of song whose mastery lies not only in the expression but in its even greater indication of what cannot be said. Such is the *genius* of knowing the unspeakable and yet being competent and compassionate enough to endure that terrific and necessary effort which art can only imply.

—Kevin McGrath, Harvard University

Start with the poem "Jet-A." This is a book by someone who has been dazed by the light and is now confronting the dark. It's an invitation for each of us to confront our shadows in our own ways. As Thomas Simmons advises, bring your own nights. These are poems to be read in the dark.

—Kenneth Fields, Stanford University Creative Writing Program

There's a deep, rumbling power to these poems, a kind of wild but tempered energy that comes only when you're lucky enough to encounter a poet capable of weaving accessible narrative with vivid, well-crafted lyricism. There's humor, too, not to mention savage intelligence paired with refreshing humanity and political conscience. In short, Simmons has gifted us with a collection spilling over with my favorite breed of poems: the kind you can teach in a classroom, lounge with on a beach, or cling to in the waiting room of an E.R., confident that at the very least, you're in good company.

—Michael Meyerhofer, author of *What To Do If You're Buried Alive*

BRING YOUR NIGHTS WITH YOU

New and Selected Poems,
1975-2015

Thomas Simmons

Volume One

SAINT JULIAN PRESS
HOUSTON

Published by
SAINT JULIAN PRESS, Inc.
2053 Cortlandt, Suite 200
Houston, Texas 77008

www.saintjulianpress.com

ISBN-13: 978-1-7320542-0-2
ISBN: 1-7320542-0-7
Library of Congress Control Number: 2018939161

Cover Art & Design: Thomas Simmons & Ron Starbuck
Author Photo: Ron Starbuck

FOR MY CHILDREN—NATE, GEORGIA,
THOMAS, HART, PETER, AND FAYE—
WITH LOVE ALWAYS

C O N T E N T S

Volume One

NEW AND RECENT POEMS

THE BODY AT REST   3

NOW   4

JET-A 5

WE MUST ALL EAT SACRIFICES 6

THE BOOK OF J   7

STONE SATCHEL 8

WINTER IN DUNBARTON 9

THESE   10

BENEDICTION 11

MARRIAGE 12

INERTIAL GUIDANCE   13

WHAT DOES IT MATTER?   15

LOVE   17

PROEM I: THE BURNING 19

THE GIFT   20

ANTI-CORRESPONDENCE   21

PLEASE, PLEASE ME LIKE I PLEASE YOU   22

HOW IT WAS 23

CHURCH MONUMENTS 24

THE AGED   25

SAINTE 26

AT ONE BEGINNING   27

SIMPLE GEOMETRY   28

HOLIDAY 30

HURQALYA 31

MUHAMMAD 33

AND I   35

EXEGESIS 37

7 JUNE 632 CE 39

THE UNIVERSE   41
I KNOW   43
THE WORD   44
ANTI-AESTHETICS 45
ALBA   46
THE SECOND DAY   47
THE BEGINNING   49
PACKING TO MOVE   50
UNCOMPREHENDING   51
ARRIVAL IN BURRAVOE   52
SHEPHERD'S PIE 54
THE NARROW ROAD TO THE FAR NORTH   56
COMFORT FOR A CHILD 57
THE PASSAGE AND THE PASSAGE OF A DAY   58
LUMINOSITY AND MAGNITUDE   59
JUST THEN   60
PARK HOUSE, BURRAVOE, YELL, ZE2 9AY 61
DEATH SPIRAL 63
LESSONS AND PRAYERS 64
FORTUNATA KÖZ   65
THE LAST POEM   67

STREET RACING

FIRST SUNDAY OF ADVENT, 1967   71
TO THE POET 72
THE HOUSE WHERE NIGHT FELL 73
THE COMPANION 74
EMBERS   75
FIREWATCHERS 76
COLLECTS   77
GUTTER, FILLED WITH RAIN   78
IMPACT   79
MY FATHER   80

NEED   81

STREET RACING   82

HEALING   83

PORTIONING THE SOUL   84

NORTH OF LAST CHANCE   85

GEMINI   86

LAST WEDNESDAY IN MARCH   87

THE WOUND AND THE CURE OF WORDS   88

HOMEBUILT   89

THE NIGHT OF THE HURRICANE   90

RAIN   91

SNOW   92

EXIT WOUND   93

"I stayed with Fortunata for one month, learning more about her ways and something about my own. She told me that for years she had lived in hope of being rescued; of belonging to someone else, of dancing together. And then she had learned to dance alone, for its own sake and for hers.
'And love?' I said.
She spread her hands and gave me a short lecture on the habits of the starfish."—Jeanette Winterson,
Sexing the Cherry (1989)

BRING YOUR NIGHTS
WITH YOU

NEW & RECENT POEMS

THE BODY AT REST

In the evening we are all of us our children,
Frightened of unconsciousness, the story's end.

This is the end of the story. Rest now.
We are inside human history, that infinitesimal

Shaft of light not yet past the Milky Way.
Forget the all in motion, forget that what we see

Shifts because we see it. Past Newton, who dreamed
Einstein but, too horrified at what he saw, dreamed

Aristotle in return, who liked things as they stayed.
The igneous rock outside his door could not be assayed

Except in its native stillness. Our stillness now.
We have fallen a long way, but see, now, how

Our mutual light recedes as our diminished sun
Appears to set. Some days it is enough to have done

Simply what we have done, and in our night
Begin to dream our journey past the speed of light.

NOW

I have been waiting years to tell you.
And now you are, as you have always been.

I see the deliberate trail you have left
Among the hostas, the day lilies, the not-yet.

The way you look down and back,
As if all our past were just that trail.

And it was. You have stepped out of all
The simulacra that you were at just

The moment I stepped out of mine.
So. Lately I have wondered at the way

Poems so imperfectly stand in—not
Something. The way poems are not.

And here you are. That was not. . .yet
All you needed was to hear me say it.

JET-A

Last night I let the kerosene lamps burn
Till dawn, that Jet-A fuel tame in the glass,
The Danforth pewter, the trimmed wick
Approximating the luxury of infinite resource—

Somewhat the way these words approximate
An infinite resource, although these words
Are three neurochemical steps away from how
My fingers, this body, know the world around me,

And that world an approximation of four forces—
But the fifth? The fifth could undo all four, for it
Approximates the remnant that is also us, or us
Without those things that Frost called "roughly zones,"

As light is light and does not bend, cold is cold,
Time runs in one direction and is constant—all this,
Now, something that might give us pause
In a dawn and not a night with miles to go,

Where sleep is likely much less a rough zone
Than a vestibule to the mansion of the absolute,
The steps winding downward and the darkness
Perfect, that howl completely drowning out the stars.

WE MUST ALL EAT SACRIFICES

Circa 940 BCE a certain woman in the court of King Solomon was in love with her memory of David, whom she had loved as a child. She wanted to write a story. In Cambridge, Mass. on July 15, 1838, the weather uncommonly fine, Ralph Waldo Emerson, who knew nothing of the woman and only the rudiments of Solomon's reign, spoke a sentence to enamored students and chiseled peers at 14 Divinity Street: *"The idioms of his language and the figures of his rhetoric have usurped the place of his truth; and churches are built not on his principles, but on his tropes."* He was referring to Jesus. He was not invited back until 1865, for the Phi Beta Kappa address. "The Divinity School Address" is smart but troubled: Emerson sought some version of the god hidden within King Solomon's court but could not model it on Jesus, who himself was an imperfect trope. The woman has come to be known in Biblical scholarship as J. She wrote of a highly personal god, to whom Abram spoke aggressively but to no avail despite his "blessing"—that god a difficult man though not a man and remarkable because he had made, well, all of this. He was not "like" David, less like Solomon, though David is the unacknowledged love interest. . .Where did god go? Again, so many baffled questions, as after Babel. . .He is here, now, as her book is here, as the beautiful women are here, as are the sacrifices we no longer dare to consume, though Sexton died a sacrifice, long before she knew He had touched the hem of her—

J, *c.* 961 BCE

J was ten, old enough to write in private and to have overheard the substance of the scrolls in the sanctum of the court, herself promised to Solomon, not yet fifteen. Late evenings she would stroll the ramparts of the temple, balancing on the narrow balustrades high above the City of David. One night that man, now aged yet still playful in his grandeur, opened the great bronze doors and walked without haste to her. *"Child,"* he said, *"For each of us there is a point of no return, and this is mine. You are of the future. Yet I have set the future in motion."* *"That was YWH's will,"* she replied without a pause. And just there was the moment when age fled. *"He has been my familiar,"* the great king said, suddenly aware that he could neither add nor take away. For then she saw how the scrolls had been inscribed as if Moses had been the great divine redactor, drawing all truth through him, and David the warrior and poet, when in truth Moses was merely as Moses had to be, and this man before her YWH's intimate. The burning bush was a warning to Moses to keep his distance; only later YWH breathed life into himself through the Psalmist. We do not know what happened next that night. But forever after, J understood that YWH was not to be as all would foretell across millennia to come, not ever unembodied. YWH had himself come out to walk with them—that brief, immeasurable distance back to the great bronze doors.

STONE SATCHEL

How finished leaves turn and shiver, eddy
As they fall, no straight path, ever.

A child asleep in its own life. The poem
By that name. All of our regions

Without mythologies. Our abject
Impoverishment. Goodwill stores.

The unmatched dishes, flatware.
Someone else's tumblers.

Nightly forgetting, every night,
But then the morning, the endeavor,

Whatever it may be. One daily goal.
The trash. The laundry. Oil change.

Used clothes for the children. Wearing
Your insignia from that war. Walking away.

Walking away with a stone satchel until
People cease to ask, to look as though

You do not belong, at last unsure
How it is that you came by your art.

WINTER IN DUNBARTON

My claim upon this place is now identical to God's,
At once nothing and all; and you, my friend,
Shedding your family privacy like an ancestral curse,
Have reached the threshold of oblivion, footnoted words:
Every anthology till doom to offer up some sample of your verse,
And this one place, still heralding all you fought, will end
Not in its privacy but in forgottenness. . .the snow-clods
Clump above the thinner clods of earth, and so rehearse

Their own predictable demise. Nothing turns to stone here.
The "Traill" in your name is what you railed against,
The evanescence of that journey, and its tense
And unparsed kinship with the Union dead, now everywhere.

Small children cry absurdly at small things—nettles on a sleeve, or
Splinters, bleeding knees—because they know as well as you
What all portends: ecstatic, slow demise of flesh, so quick
To burn, molten eyes relenting till the little we receive
Slinks into the unknown. Your hero then a preacher who
Created the most fierce vision of how routinely we deceive
Ourselves and one another, Hell as far from fiction
As you are now from us. In the end they banished him to grieve

Among the western settlers, used to detritus, and the native tribes.
Old friend, I summon you: what binds us is what recollection
Left you, those last two years in Cambridge, elder of one season
So permanently dark and cold. Forgiveness came among the grebes

And gulls of Stonington. The ground, thankless; no selectmen now
To remember those selectmen; no one, not even I, can hear
Those chattering dead. Your nemesis was right: this secrecy
Is not the porch of spirits lingering. It is the tomb of Jesus,
Where he lay. And you as well: can you imagine this is how
It would become, this something that is not you here
Beside me, as real as the snow? I witness
Your resurrection—one secrecy that time will still allow.

THESE

The way I know you now, as perhaps I always did:
Through conjurings—as if that were fair, as if anyone
Had the right to make a person from a person, though all
Do. Also we resist, as we must—thus the constant

Hue and cry. For once I would like you to see me,
Shorn of rumour, and I you, shorn of fantasy.
There would be no poems. Our speech might be
About common things, how thin you seem, how

The years that were a kind of triumph in reality
Were unkind. I can feel a lie from far off,
Having lived that larger-than-lie childhood,
But hope, hope is my weakness. For myself

I would lay hope aside, when the time came,
And simply walk with you, attentive to the wind
In your long hair, your words, the way my eyes
Have begun to fail in the twilight, so that I cannot

Be sure what I am seeing. By then I think
You would know what to do. The love was always
There, however filled with fear, or anger. These are
Last year's words. There is nothing more to see.

BENEDICTION

The things that stay, stay. Those that pass,
Pass. Pointless to cry after them, although we must:

Our nature, after all. No need to make excuse
For what is real. But when we run ourselves

Into the ground, that is the benediction, that taste
Of dirt in the mouth, the sudden damp and chill:

'Wake up! Wake up!" the earth is crying urgently,
Though not to us, but that is what we hear.

And if we do not wake, whose fault is that?
We were made for sleep. Sleepwalking, we pursue

The real and the unattainable, the antithetical:
Days away from rest, we crave oblivion.

After brief sleep, which scarcely yields, I wake
To the echoed blessing of my kind, the one

When the running man fell and the ground spoke.
I take from that this truth: one voice to match my own.

MARRIAGE

I was thinking about marriage. . .
Not in the way we tend to practice it
These days, a little haphazardly,
But as a vocation in which energy,

Converted to mass, converts back
To energy. . .Which I think is what we do
When we pass through death. I always hated
That expression, "passing," because Christian

Scientists used it since "death" was too
Graphic. But, turning to David Sadava's
Life: The Science of Biology, I am touched
Over and over again by his simple

Lovingkindness: "a chemical bond
Is an attractive force that links two atoms
Together in a molecule." "A covalent bond
Forms when two atoms attain stable electron

Numbers in their outermost shells by
Sharing one or more pairs of electrons."
Slowly, over Philip Larkin's eons,
We acquired mass. . .I think about

Becoming a Catholic, my love of the idea
Of "Mass," the Eucharist with its
Transubstantiation, in which matter
Becomes energy becomes—us:

We bond with what now lies
Beyond time, its own gravitational force
Pulling us harder, and harder, through marriage
And back, so many cells already shed, back home.

INERTIAL GUIDANCE

Strange to think that where we go in space depends
On how we know the Earth, and what each move portends,

A motion that returns us to the body. How do you know
Where you are? In the years of genocide, we saw

With too little awe the way an Indian scout could sense
A trail from the scent of the earth, vibrations over distance

Seemingly unimaginable, or a private vision of terrain.
Our instruments have taught us somewhat to refrain

From judging what we cannot see. I myself have an internal
Sense of time that rarely varies, continuously computing all

The variables of barometric pressure, speed, distraction:
Looking at a clock at 9 A.M., I know at 1:05 PM

That it is 1:05. I share this intuition with my four-year-old,
Peter, who cannot read a clock yet feels that what he's told

Is what it is. Funny that the first key to inertial navigation
Was a child's toy, the top, creating mild amusement as it spun

Fiercely at first, impervious to the shifting angle of the floor
Until, like us at the end of day or life, it just leaned over

From the wear of friction. We know that tops existed
In classical Greece and Rome, in China. John Serson

Added a gimbal to the spinning axis and we had a test,
In 1743, for knowing the horizon in a heavy fog or mist.

How late Johann Bohnenberger developed "The Machine,"
1817, two gimbals around a spinning axis, and even then

We waited until 1852, when Leon Foucault built what we call,
Now, a "gyroscope": he used it for his students as a model

Of the earth's rotation. The great paradox—something that would
Hold position, yet register each shift in angle, dip, or bend:

Combine two gyroscopes with two accelerometers, a primitive
Mechanical computer, and a vessel, and the world now lives

Inside that "black box," deducing the position of the body
From the angles of its motion and its minute, unsteady

Speeding-up or slowing-down. I wish I could have seen
That light dawn, shortly before World War II, when sane,

Methodical scientists suddenly realized they could go anywhere,
Even into space, and never get lost. Bombs falling, and the glare

Of chaos, but still they saw the embodied miracle of freedom:
We could go. We ourselves would wait for Wernher von Braun

But all of his inventions and refinements rested on this new thing,
Inertial guidance, which we had had as humans in the coding

Of our DNA. How little we know of what we know. . .When I say,
Unsentimentally, but with such gratitude, "I love you,"

Or, more contentiously, "The universe rests on love," you may
Hear one thing while I mean another: look closely.

My iPhone has a "microelectromechanical system," MEMS,
That would enable me, confronted with the catastrophic loss

Of computational power in a jet airplane, to land that craft
In the worst weather using only my knowledge of old ADF

Technology and my phone. . .Or I could just install
The Garmin aircraft moving map app and make it simple.

The gyroscope *per se* is obsolete. Yet I can always find
One on my desk, to entertain or fascinate a certain kind

Of child or guest, and more still, to remind myself of how
We must invent to learn from our inventions what we knew.

WHAT DOES IT MATTER?

"Freud interprets this poignant vision as the father's wish fulfillment, bringing the child back to life in much the same extremity as Lear holding the dead Cordelia in his arms. It hardly required the French mystagogue Jacques Lacan to indicate that Freud's minimalism here is insupportable. . .For the burning child is the astral body, and not to read him as a prophetic image is to miss him."—Harold Bloom, *Omens of Millennium*

"Everything brave has to start somewhere"—Sara Seager, Professor of Astrophysics, MIT

At first, 51 Pegasi b, in 1995—radial velocity the mathematical
Method to detect a gravitational shift, an exoplanet around a star.
Then the greatest thrill of science outside the lone-genius myth—
The heated research rush, coincidence if you believe that, the Kepler

Spacecraft observing in 2014, 550 light-years away, a one-percent
Drop in light on Kepler-186f, reading light as music, interplays
Of basic molecules implying, perhaps, an atmosphere, or rain,
Blue skies. . .And then another (leaving aside the other 298
      elsewhere)

Orbiting Proxima Centauri, closest kin to us in light-years. Thus
We confront contingent worth, or "accidental" worth: no reason
To disbelieve Zoroaster or Karma Lingpa, or Ibn 'Arabi,
No reason to doubt resurrection is continuous and takes place

Not here but in what the late 17th-century British believers
Called "Eden," what we might call "imaginal reality," not in the least
Imaginary. Our reality, unchosen, present. Where are you now?
Are you ecstatic? Unhingeing in your grief? If you believe millennia

Of gnosis, you need do nothing, though compassion for the joyous
As well as the impurely crushed is essential, because a consequence
Of the seed and root of love; still, the imaginal will come for you
In the end, when forgiveness of sins is perpetual. Everything here,

Thus, a kind of contingent worth. . .But how can we not go?
"Contingent" does not diminish, "imaginal" cannot but transfigure—
Would you have wanted not to see the Grand Canal, the Himalaya,
The MIT blackboard covered in formulae to explain the atmospheres

Of light—I'm didactic here because elsewhere I'm lyrical and lovely,
Having earned this, near our small, contingent sun. Already we intuit
    what
Niayesh Afshordi and João Magueijo so elegantly laid out in the
    Physical
Review—not even light, now, earning its unmade claim to constancy.

LOVE

"For he that dwelleth in love dwelleth in God, and God in him." John I: 6:14

For tho it be a Maxime in the Scholes, That there is no Lov of a thing unknown; yet I have found, that Things unknown have a Secret Influence on the Soul: and like the Centre of the Earth unseen, violently Attract it. . . .Do you not feel yourself Drawn with the Expectation and Desire of som Great Thing?—Thomas Traherne, Century I: ii (c. 1669)

Now a scientific curio, David Cowan's
        Mind Underlies Spacetime: An Idealistic Model
                Of Reality. Belmont Press, 1975. Physicist
And Christian Scientist, Cowan was my idol.
Even then, though, there were problems:

Mary Baker Eddy listed seven synonyms for God:
        Mind, Soul, Spirit, Life, Truth, Love, Principle. Why, then,
                Should Cowan's equations raise that one above
        The rest? Not hard to guess: we yearn, I suppose, to see
Intelligence, above all beneath phenomena, seen

And unseen. But not me. Bereft from early on,
        I sought not that "Mind" of Cowan, nor Thoreau's "Truth,"
                But rather love. Mind was elegance,
        Truth either was or was not; love, without fail,
Was transformative. Alone, love guaranteed it never left us

Where or as it found us. (Who said that? Mary Baker Eddy,
        Of course.) For one so wounded in what Ezra Pound
                Once called "the loneliness and partiality"
        Of the single self, love was always the key.
Yet, decades on, with death now arguably closer than love,

I have learned other questions: so many possible permutations
        Of the six primary elements, and a universe
                Comprised of matter antithetical to us, regions
        We could not enter as ourselves, and forces enormous
And infinitesimal beyond anything that Robert Hookes could see:

I posit now that love is biological, mammalian, evolving
        As we evolved. . .Just watch the shift from Babylonian

To Abraham and Isaac, Lot's daughters, Jesus,
Or the *trobar clus,* Dante's *Vita Nuova*; in the West we've
Come far through the past that made our love a yearning best

When unfulfilled, imagined into being as an affirmation
Of the self as it transforms itself. . .
And God. . .It comforts me, ironically,
To think of Him as a local God, Newtonian and sad,
With all of Traherne's yearning. . .desire is key

And He Himself, if gendered, may have foreseen that we'd
Eclipse him millennia down the road. Milton
Knew even more than he was willing to say:
God was lonely. And we, in our many rounds
Of loneliness, may call on God and feel comforted,

Not because his abundant love carries us through crises,
But because he yearns for us. He would contact us
If he could, if he could once again trust Gabriel.
Love may be stronger than death. But one day we will say
Good-bye, even to him. Still: if I am loyal, you know why.

PROEM I: THE BURNING

Once a day I venture out to the market
        full-body Patagonia underwear long sleeves   long pants
            No one can see   how my skin still peels

Nothing will stop it   I return to the hospital
        every other day   for triage treatment   compassion
           "We've never seen   anything like this"

But how can that be?   Between *De Rerum Natura*
        and *De Amores* this body should be in its way
           normative   each touch a scar   each scar's

Skin peeling away   and the bloody subcutaneous tissue
        unstoppable   as adoration is unstoppable:
           Fine—call it "LOVE"—

How early—Mary at eight—our parents broke us up
        after a month   because we were talking nightly
           over the phone and she was Catholic

Names and dates—until now the in-patient burn unit
        but I cannot. Thus this *Art of Uncourtly Love*
           Which is called *And Then*

Because it is what comes after and before *Now*,
        Because every sliver of skin is a sliver of a heart
           That does not exist.

II. The Gift

Some here cut. I myself lower myself
Onto the flame, hand, arm, for the most-hot
Navy blue a certain ingenuity, odd angle

Of the torso, buttocks, thigh. They admit me
Because obviously I have been in repeated
Accidents but see how my body resembles

The intentional, the ones here who did this
To feel pain, to feel alive. We do not speak
Of love, not ever. Yet evenings, darkness

Looming, I roam the silent halls until
My tortured roommate falls asleep to music—
Then the tiny bedside light, the paper and pen,

This. Each concealed wound must be a gift
In language, or there is no point. We do not
Speak of love. Twice a day the dressings

Come off, sanitary napkins tossed in
Biohazard. Twice a day I see how my body
Responds. At night, these words, their kin.

ANTI-CORRESPONDENCE

The Third Temple presaged late nature now whose leaves shatter like glass or melt in the liquid heat, what happens when the covenant and arc have both vanished, the city of Sikri a ruin without water and the populace to Agra or Lahore, empire slowly "riding the metamorphoses" to ruin. We can ride only so far before the absence of the covenant reduces Ovid to a guess. With whom have you agreed? Friends of brother's friends down by the restrooms in the park, the circle of secret evergreens, the pulling-down of pants, pain like a long-in-the-future angiogram without anesthetic administered this time in the anus—overwhelming even the "why"—and the not-walking, the two weeks of paralysis. How I would love to believe in the grotesque: that at least might be some kind of covenant, risking the body to its own horrors. Now I mostly watch the people come and go in their magnificent manner of bringing the body under fascistic control, no whisper of errant hair nor failed 5K time until the rebellion of cancer, the hideous replication of the heedless: things that frightened and repelled me for years are my fair play now, exotic unguents and the soft fluids following, ecstasy upon ecstasy, however temporary, however over-and-again when I know that life outside the body exists in source code, Pascal, Assembly, and by analogy in quadratic equations, special relativity of a universe that gives us this place only because it is ours to take, *De Rerum Natura,* Titus Lucretius Carus.

PLEASE, PLEASE ME LIKE I PLEASE YOU

It began slowly and in her thrill she was sweating and starting to tremble, the small ring of trees like a temple, though she was not there. Yet as they began and he knew with relief this was true and he would come they slowly turned, she on top and her sweat running down to his abdomen and he saw as from a slight distance how he began to shimmer until despite it all he became

$$\beta = \frac{v}{c} = \frac{(z+1)^2 - 1}{(z+1)^2 + 1}$$

redshift: recessional velocity relative to the speed of light and she by contrast of climax became molecular, acetylcholine receptor at the intensity of synapse $> 10,000/\mu m^2$ and so then they were both objectified or he had objectified them, if he had—long ago someone had arrogated his body. He fought his way back because it was what he knew, inside the consciousness that was not a simulacrum only because it was not shared, because it was his for a time and if it was hers, when there would be a "her," she would tell him, privately, even if tiny CCTV lenses in the trees put it all over the web and later people snickered in public, watching in airports, bus stations, to the ire of others, the whole narrative lost—well—they had had what they had had, moving beyond imagination toward the edge of the universe and creating, just there, that new synaptic link, that thing, meaning.

HOW IT WAS

Night fell by the river. And after,
And before, the same. No one saw

Grey creatures without a name:
They were just there. Then gone.

And then again—but wait—what I want
Is to tell you things you haven't

Yet seen, which is a way of saying:
Those things will take away your mind.

They will. You know this. That will
We daily summon, counter-animal.

The animal prevails in the small cries
By the river, the chirps of ecstasy

Or fear—think what you will, these words
Are not about a thought. They are the birds

That Jesus made, uncaring, never to alight
Yet lighting here beside me now. The slight

Nuance of a moan or sigh, the little token
Of not-being-witnessed, the unseen.

CHURCH MONUMENTS

To go among the dead you must know sorrow well
Yet live outside of sorrow, in domains of multiplicity.
The monuments are key, oracular in the dark:
We rarely realize we choose what we want to hear,
As they begin nocturnal colloquies of possibility
There, when the unseen shines. "I dwell in possibility"—
One of the those seemingly casual, almost comic
Revelations from E.D., who understood true ravishment
Through metaphor, the sea driving her to come and come
Until, just there, the edge of the *solid town*. . .And she, too,
With a stone to tell, in language purely image, almost too
Many versions of the everything that might have been,
And is now, right by right, though she has portioned out
Herself to all minute particulars, perceived and unperceived,
Here, in the quiet garden of this cemetery night.

THE AGED

Slowly the aged return from their dark portals
And stand silent at the perimeter. What was it
We wanted to ask—the nature of each portal,
Each new evanescence, our own inattentiveness—
That pettiness—they have seen now those things

They cannot tell us, for it would not matter:
We grasp them only when we are there,
Which is why a poem is also merely
A motion toward, why my love is absolute
And my death unshareable, and age—

I begin to see—not something out from the dark:
Its difference. Its unlikeness. The un-wisdom of youth
To whom above all wisdom should become. The same
Name but a different person entirely, not any cell
Or neuron as before. . .Only a tapestry of stories,

Sideways turned to the width of a thread that soon
Will weave itself into others, until whatever it was
Is there with nothing in its stead. The darkness
Is not the threat, nor silence, but what never was,
The missed turns, that rusted wreckage by the road.

SAINTE

After Stephane Mallarmé

The glass almost conceals; yet within,
That faded gilt of the sandalwood
Viol, luminous as before with mandolin
Or flute, refusing to be hidden;

And there, the pale saint pouring
Her biblical flood, the ancient liturgy
Of the Magnificat, still streaming
As if old vespers or compline were worthy:

Apart from us, now, in monstrance,
Waiting, echoing that angel's orison
Whose vision is his night flight, just askance
At her upraised finger on the string

Where, without the ancient sandalwood
Or the ancient liturgy, she balances
Herself upon the mortal truth of no sound,
Musician of all our silences.

AT ONE BEGINNING

"In this Letter, we revisit a class of VSL [variable speed of light] models. . .in which there are two non-conformal metrics, one for matter and another for gravity, so that light and other massless matter particles travel faster than gravity. Conditions for the observational success of such models have been identified."— *Niayesh Afshordi and João Magueijo,* Physical Review

Light is love. The dark is love
Before it met us. The dark is entranced.

Some of it is static. Some of it is not.
It does not concern itself with temperature.

Yet comes a temperature anomaly—
$13,000^{36}$ Celsius—yes, you can imagine—

Massless particles under such release.
It is no longer a constant. It has felt the presence

Of the dark and it has responded. Suddenly
Everything is there—everything you knew

You wanted, everything you didn't. It is there
Because of you, of us, although we are uncreated,

Unable to withstand. Yet we are. Everything—
Mostly it looks stable, as it did at some beginning,

Or just after. Love cools. It simulates reality.
But that is its look. We look to the stars

For answers. The answer lies in a tiny
Thermal fluctuation in a vacuum.

SIMPLE GEOMETRY

Even now I catch myself as I was, when left alone, brilliant child,
        five, say, with a penchant for trees
And angles, "Congruent Parts of Congruent Triangles Are
        Congruent," CPCTC, and my height as radius,
3.5 feet x 2 x π or 3.1415926 for a circumference of
        21.9911482 feet—my world, whether at the top
Of the old dogwood out back or in the center of my room,
        designing a Matchbox town out of cardboard
And Scotch tape. It was enough—Stay Back. That was the rule. Let
        us not revisit   here the early trauma

Or what I oh-so-reluctantly now call—well, no—only to myself

Stay   Back//

With almost eleven feet of ambient room—call it eleven—you could
        go anywhere:
Dogfighting at the top of the tree was fine, Venice was fine, I liked
        Mars, I like playing inside
The rings of Saturn. Things changed: in spring of sixth grade a close
        friend, who wore mini-
Skirts and went over to the high school after, stopped
        wearing underwear, though always that chaste slip.
It was another two years before I connected wet dreams with how
        Sunday School explained that fucking
Placed us outside of God's Love. No cause-effect: a purely
        random, meaningless universe. Home. I was in Geometry
        then:

$$A = \pi r^2$$

I began to calculate the area. The area of my life. How much I had, in
        inches, millimeters, feet.
Some decades it expanded; then it began to contract: now—well—
        these nights Venus actually appears
High above the moon, and the moon 240,000 miles away—now,
        paradoxically,
I live inside my child's town. I find it strange, Newton
        calculating binomials at 22.

What was he solving for, really? Interesting to ponder his area: you
      know what
Happened then—the house, the name, the Royal Society.

HOLIDAY

Because of an intentional overdose of the antidepressant Remeron I was permitted the journey to a non-existent town on the southern border of Iran by the Red Sea, where a large, concentric resort encircles a central observatory. Only those who have received the necessary pre-vision can attend, and so the crowd is congenial, unconcerned with the terrible dangers of the day, gentle. They have come to listen to the lives of creatures on some of the 3,000 exoplanets in the Milky Way and the more distant galaxies. Among the many comforts here—complete absence of haste, abundant food, and no fixed schedule—one comes to separate false prophets from the true: Isaiah was in part false, part true; Joseph Smith was false; Mary Baker Eddy was false. Jeanette Winterson, on the other hand, was true. On Proxima Centauri b—though, yes, this was long ago now—the people did live in floating houses without floors and walked on the air. On 51 Pegasi b, such precise radio signals as we have pulled in from our Kepler and the others show a castle with 12 princesses, escaping in a different way each night to perform their exotic dances. Not the least of the joy here is discovering how to "hear" a radio signal as if it were, say, a completely comprehensive code: think *The Matrix*. On Kepler-186f, the creatures were obsessed paradoxically with human history in the 21st century, part *Hunger Games*, part *Firefly*, and so there is a rule here that only the astronomers with at least three previous visits can listen, because it is cripplingly easy for humans, even those gifted with vision, to give in to despair, and—because John of Patmos was also not a false prophet—one would not want to listen for long hours at what will have to occur before we really begin to bend time and space, our remnant traveling outward.

HURQALYA

"The cities are the souls which have become attached to material bodies, or else the faculties which have their seat in the latter. It seems, therefore, that the author is comparing the faculties to the inhabitants of these cities and is calling the inhabitants themselves cities, as when he says, 'The city has sought refuge with God,' meaning thereby the inhabitants."—Ibn Kammüna in Shihabuddin Suhrwawardi, Hurqalya

How many years it took to understand there was no rush to come,
       apart from those rare
Mutual explosions of embodied need, the slow, slower
       caresses all along your length, pausing, yes,
At areola, the shift from buttocks to thigh and then reverse, the cleft
       at the base of the spine,
Insistently just outside the labia and then just there, at the top, ever
       so slowly in, until you began
To shake from the intensity and then, yes, it was time to come,

I come to tell you that that is what the holy cities are like, each one of
       us a sad city cut off from Hurqalya,
Which has been calling us, calling our bodies and, despite what we
       may have been told, affirming
Rather than rejecting the immensities of our too-infrequent
       pleasure amid the squalor, affirming
The rightness of the body in its rightful place. Why should a child
       feel compelled, on a certain day,
To begin to build a city on the floor of his room, and then
       another, and another—

Three years, all told, each city entirely different, as if from
       different planets? What did he know,
He who knew little of sex? He knew that one day he should look
       back at that child and marvel,
Just as I am marveling now, that it was all there, despite the
       accidents of history and the terrible losses,
All of it in preparation for this poem of departure, this
       invitation for you, too, to claim
Your birthright as both inhabitant and city, the rightful
       circumference and area

Of those two π equations, so simple that a smart child knows
        them even before she knows
Her numbers, needing to know for no particular earthly reason but
        for the realization
Years or decades later, whether she is taken by force of evil or natural
        age, this was all
Building toward the slow, blinding vision that there was, after
        all, a purpose, that her cities
Became in the end one city which is her at the birth of her first
        ecstasy.

MUHAMMAD

And the Lord God was walking in the garden in the cool of the day.
          Comforted Adam
And incomparable Eve he expected to greet. But instead he heard a
          groaning, as of a woman
In travail with child, which could not possibly yet have
          happened. Around the corner by the tree,
He saw a man on his knees, in great distress. He had with him
          implements the Lord God
Had never seen. *"Who art thou,"* demanded the incredulous,
          omniscient Lord.

"Art thou that Satan whom I have cast down?" The man turned and
          looked. *"No man shalt*
see my face and live," saith the Lord of *The Book of J*, 1200 years in the
          future. "I am that man,"
Saith the man. "I have come to record the teachings of the Lord to
          those my people,"
And he gestured toward a desert to the south. The God of Past,
          Present, and Future was incensed.
"You have no right here," the Lord raged. *"I shall strike you down."*

"Strike me then," saith the Man. And the Lord did not. Could not.
          Then the man spake.
"Almost was I persuaded that Al-Lat was the Lord," he replied. "But
          now I see somehow
That what I thought was heaven is riddled with demi-gods and idols.
          My scriptures are
Corrupt, and some I must renounce. There is but one God, and Allah
          is His name." At that point
The Lord God vanished, as did the garden, and Muhammad found
          himself in a cave

Of light, the golden light without attribute—call it "prophecy,"
          "comfort," "love to right
All wrongs"—none of these would be wrong, though none right. It
          was 1900 years in the future
From what had just occurred. Muhammad was bone-tired. He went
          back to the village

With his scroll, his pen and ink. In his new tunnel vision,
     nevertheless out of the corner of his eye
He saw the child Ayesha uncupping her hands and lifting the
     butterflies aloft.

AND I

And I with my ordinary name and unremarkable background set
        forth into the companionable blackness
Of the Universal Night, as before I have often done, life in the caves
        of the day having reached
Its logical conclusion. Neither meditation nor vocation, and yet, yes,
        a calling, the Universal Night
You may enter through the end of your street where the
        streetlight is burned out or where
In the cemetery is the secret entrance to the park of a thousand trails,

Except that you cannot get lost in the Universal Night because, once
        through the portal,
All the trails disappear as does all anxiety about whether,
        philosophically speaking, there should be
A trail or not. After that, nothing is up to you, though that, too, is
        not quite correct: you know
You are there for a reason. Many times nothing will come of it. You
        will find yourself
In your bed on a sunny morning, only for a brief moment
        mourning the sun.

Prophecy tells you what it is you will see when, finally, you see it, for
        the tales do not vary
Over the course of almost 300 years, before the Falling Off and the
        retreat of the light
Into the pages of books. At some point, after much study, I began to
        become aware in my evening readings
That the books were rippling, the words mirrors, light and darkness
        and not text
Playing before me. Then I began to walk. That is what I do, now.

The Universal Night is wherever you are summoned, at times eons
        away, but at one specific time
The reversal occurs: the night would have to be there for the Man of
        Light finally to speak
Kindly to you, asking you what it is that you already know, and thus
        you will know that you,

That all of us, are within a solar system with a sun among 400 billion
     suns in the neighborhood
Because the kind voice awaits all of us for the investiture that is
     uniquely yours.

EXEGESIS

Ellipses and ruptures: life and the children of life, stories,
Not the least Genesis 3: 23-25. Beloved of the mystical exegetes
Close to the court of Charles II, the verses have a God who drives
        out
"The man," Eve unmentioned, "to till the ground from whence
He was taken." No mention of a fall, or falling, or being cast down:

Furthermore, if Adam was to till the ground from whence
He was taken, the ground of Eden must be everywhere, or
        somewhere,
Outside of Eden, despite the flaming angels at the East Gate.
Thus they reasoned; 120 years later, Blake had his own reasons
To build "Jerusalem in England's green and pleasant land."

I climbed trees—still do, at 60. I never fell, though friends did,
A broken leg, a broken arm, eternal badge of bravery. I liked
To drop things: how fast would they go? How long would
It take? Eventually I came across 9.8m/2/2, and that lasted
For a time. But then, of course, the question more like life:

Accelerated upward, how long would it take to fall? Or rather:
How hard would one land? Thus: $v_f = v_i + at$, where v_f is the final
Velocity, v_i the initial, plus acceleration times time. Bam: things
Thrown upward come down hard, and I watched this over and over,
A little below the angels in a dogwood with a stopwatch, one other
        equation,

And some estimates. Just as well to be playing, not to know
For a few more years that this would summarize all of life
Until such time as one could leave the world in the way
The equations of special relativity leave it, in the way
DNA goes down to its unrecognizable roots. Late in the night,

Just before dreaming: the body in space, once accelerated,
Moving it would seem on its own without interference, without
Fate, simply moving, and only a wise soul knowing it had already

Come under the faint gravitational pull of a star still barely
As bright as our own sun, the leave-taking absolute, as it must be.

7 JUNE 632 CE

"[Ibn 'Arabi explained:] The secret of the creation of the palm tree made from the remainder of the clay from which Man himself was created. And, of the clay from which his own 'sister' [the palm tree] was molded, there was still an invisible remainder, the equivalent of a sesame *seed, no more. But this very fact conveys the meaning that there is no common measure between the expanse of sensory space and that which begins at the point where the directions of sensory space come to an end."—Henry Corbin,* Spiritual Body and Celestial Earth

And so it came to pass that Muhammad summoned Suhrawardi and
        Ibn 'Arabi from the 12th and 13th centuries, CE,
And they found themselves walking beside him, on the main road
        into Yahtrib. The route
Was uncommonly deserted. Only the day before, Muhammad
        lay seemingly comatose
In his bed, Ayesha beside him. Today Muhammad was cross. *"You
        have not kept the Ayah,"*
He accused them. And they, having seen one another in the Imaginal,
        were silent.

Then: *"The Revelation was complete,"* Ibn 'Arabi said. *"But even you were
        forced to renounce some
Of what you had written. The Revelation, though complete, could not possibly
        have been finished, for then
What would have been left for us to do? We have followed the Ayah precisely
        where it has led us."* Muhammad
Walked with a powerful wooden staff, made of Lebanese cedar, and
        he raised it as if to strike
A fatal blow far into the future. But a certain Jew, hard by the
        side of the road,

Unnoticed with his broken wagon wheel and his quiet
        donkey, stepped suddenly between them.
Suhrawardi instinctively raised his arm to protect the Prophet.
        At that moment, the staff
And the arm of the Jew and of Suhrawardi crossed, and just then
        lightning split the jet-black sky

And when the sun returned after an unknown time, no one could see
    the bottom of the pit.
Suhrawardi: *"Just so has Ibn 'Arabi spoken the truth. For this here, in the
    clay of the earth,*

*Is Universal Night, as we have seen, and the Jew was the Man of Light whom
    Gabriel spoke of to you*
 *In Hira. This was not a miracle. It was the work of the three of us in consonance
    with the living Ayah."*
The Jew had vanished. Ibn 'Arabi and Suhrawardi returned to
    Persia. Old in his confusion,
Muhammad sank to the side of the crowded road, and the crowd
    marveled and carried him home.
The next day, Ayesha by his side, Muhammad died.

THE UNIVERSE

*"Just because a machine doesn't think like a human, does that mean that it is not
'thinking'"?*
—Alan Turing, 1952

Posit four realities: neutron stars. cosmic supermagnets. Einstein
        pulsars. And those
"Prisons for light," black holes—about which we can say only that
        "our theories of physics
Are not sophisticated enough to explain what happens in these."[1]
What these most have in common is that they exist at the limits of
        our conscious awareness.

Comic, it would seem, to raise the question of the Earth on the back
        of an elephant on the back
Of a giant tortoise—"But what does the tortoise rest on?" Yet it is
        one of the most sophisticated questions,
And entirely relevant: what is the substratum of consciousness? Our
        answer: neurons,
Axons, synapses, indebted to species-wide and individual DNA. But
        given that,

We confront the miracle that the question itself is wrong: we attain
        consciousness because
Of a substratum, but so do other substrata, and we have no evidence
        that consciousness itself
Depends on these: they only bring it into an awareness of itself.

And yet it moves so freely beyond the pages of a book, the
        unrepeatable visions of Valentinus
In the second century CE, nothing more to say, a
        superconductivity of affirmation and perception
That among other things yields a new dignity to the 1960's cliché
        "mind-blowing"—for, yes,

---

[1] Govert Schilling, *Deep Space* (New York: Black Dog and Leventhal
Publishers, 2014), p. 109

That is what minds are for. To be blown. The substratum will
      go, one way

Or another, and there we will be, though "where" is incalculable, and
      there is no guarantee
That you will be you, that I will be me, nor, to be fair, any
      reason we should care.

I KNOW

The times you curl into me wordlessly, fetal yet fully here,
Are the times you cannot bear that what I might be arguing
Is a lack of intrinsic meaning—how hard you've tried to be kind,
How you have loved, how you have grieved your losses, watching
As I grieved mine. That that is all some kind of illusion—no—
Things make their own meaning in their own time. Few things
More fragile than a human. My father a Naval officer, I know
The tropes of strength, the absurd lies about slogging through

"It all"—as if there were no limit, as if soldiers and vets did not
Go off for a reason. The war drove my father mad. I theorize
Because in my life there was too much loss, and if that outweighs
The neutron star of love, then you and I there meet—there is
No point. I confess: I want it both ways: your curling beside me
In your need, sharing my own, and I expecting still the revelation.

THE WORD

One day a child came to her father.
"Father," she said, "I am tired of words.
Nothing ever changes and the stories are
Already old." Say she was 10. He gazed upon her,
Then motioned toward the door. Wordless, they
Put on coats, hats, gloves, boots, and walked
Into the snow. About an hour passed. Town
Turned to country. They walked through a mottled
Fallow field, remnants of corn stalks like 1,000
Tiny trails, and into a wood, where the snow eddied
At the trunks of the old-growth oaks and maples.
The wood was still, the birds quiet. Some slivers
Of sun broke through the clouds. She slid
Her gloved hand inside his. They walked home.
When they had undone all the warm things
And laid them aside, he glanced at her,
Almost too intentional, and she understood
What he was asking. She shook her head. No,
She had not missed it, any of it, nor did she
Wish to recount. It had been enough, the sound
Of boots in the snow, the quiet, the sudden sun,
Her hand in his. There was no mother, brother, sister.
From then on the house was silent. Even at the town
School, after awhile, people stopped calling. One day
When the sheriff came by, the house was empty.

ANTI-AESTHETICS

The old distinctions blur—sublimity not a category
Sir Joshua Reynolds defined but rather the thing
Becoming at once itself and another, the undulant
Low hills of Burravoe and Ulsta embodying wind
As much as earth, and the strange sound, part quiet
Howl, part crackle, coming off the depths between
Ulsta and Toft. The ferry holds 45 cars. The slip at Yell
Is as unprepossessing as an alms-beggar. Come home.
Beauty is where the world enters your body through
Each cell and capillary, the wind one with your heart
And your heart to aery thinness beat in the coarse grass
Where the ruddy colts graze, and that bus from the 1950's,
Where practically nothing is original. In time everything
Becomes what it was not; here, no threat but a living
Purpose, how you move through a day, the often-theorized
Multiple selves not theory here but the private affirmation
That you could not possibly, no, not ever have been alone.

ALBA

Her name was Alba, rooted in the land. We rowed
Back round to the southeast of Samphrey, past some ruins
And a pond not quite connected to the sea at north and south.
At the sandy beach there we hauled out, and across the moor,
Her long hair the color of wind in the dark, and the wind in the dark
Her hair, we came to a small cottage of masonry and slate, with a fire
In its place and a rough stone floor, densely-woven carpets
Marking the living room, dining room. Up the ladder to the loft
Was the bed, with its small window looking south toward the deeper
Darkness of that sudden depth of sea.
                                    He thought she was about
To say, "And you feel like you've been here before," but he caught
Her look that said she had already finished that conversation
On her own. "Did you know I was coming?" He asked.
She turned her back to him, opening some cheese
Wrapped in wax and paring an apple, drawing down
Some cider from an upper shelf. "How old do you think
I am?" She said. "You said you were 27." "But what do
You think?" He took a seat by the fire. "I think you are
Exactly my age," he said. She turned and smiled, bringing
The food and drink to the small table between their chairs.
"Think again," she said. *"Before Adam was, I am.'* You as well,
You whom I have watched over the decades, reducing yourself
Almost to ruin. I did not know whether you would find your way."

I thought. "I thought you knew everything," I said. "I thought,
When I awoke, that you had brought me here." She laughed.
"What good would it do to know everything?" she said.
"Tomorrow we will begin our exploration, until every inch
Of this island is re-inscribed in your heart. Then over
To Yell, and Burravoe." Call it what you will—the eighth day,
Say, or perhaps the twilight of the sixth, God retreating
In a sudden shock that gravitations beyond his creating
Were pulling his creation in some new way, and not even
The Tree of the Knowledge of Good and Evil would be
Enough to save Him from what He had set in motion.

THE SECOND DAY

As for the night, there were no words for it,
And when he awoke that early day in April, near 10 AM,
Dawn was deep in the marrow of the land. Her touch
Had gone everywhere, caresses *in excelsis* as if his flesh
Had been his soul turned outward and forever alone till then:
He came to her almost as after-thought of ecstasy that began
With her face hovering above his, her jet-black hair laving his face,
Neck, and shoulders, her breath both scent and scenting,
At some point encompassing his body. By the window, an old pair
Of Benelux binoculars, dented from hard use: he looked out.
She was there, where the bay met the North Sea, in the dory,
Grey on grey and the jet black lying back just a bit against
The starboard gunwale: adrift, the oars stored athwart,
She was reading. Yet at his incredulous gaze she looked up,
Turned, a mile distant, reset the oars in the locks and began
To row in. Not so much that she was strong, but that she
Had never ceased this kind of labor which was second nature,
Never from childhood. By the time he had dressed and got down
To the sandy beach, she was close to hauling out. What was he
To her—he knew and didn't know: there was evening and there
Was morning, the seventh day, but this was rest unlike any
He had known. He pulled the bow ashore with the painter,
Then the two of them together, pulling the dory well up the sand:
The book was Ibn 'Arabi, *Alone with the Alone,* from the 13th century,
From Persia. "I have eggs in the icebox, and cheese of course,"
She said as if no time had passed from their childhoods.
"Make us two omelettes, and a light snack with the cheese
And the bread from the breadbox, and then we will go
To the top of the island and work our way down in slow
Spirals." "Why—" he began, but before it left his lips it had become
A multifoliate question, although at first he had only wanted to know
One thing, which she knew. "To be a true pair," she replied,
"You have to know what it means to be alone in an animate world,
Which is not where you have lived, though you have seen it
In dreams. You saw it last night, when in dreams you sought
In vain in that huge library in California for the book

I am holding now in my hand. You asked, you looked, but no one
Knew. It was not I who planted the dream. The island planted the dream.
I simply wanted to see what it was you thought you didn't know."
And so they went in, the wind light on her hair and her hair
Black light in the wind, and on her shoulders 'Arabi's own full
Attention, he as we might say "back from the dead"—though that
Would be wrong, he who had never died, who lived adjacent in the flashes
Of dawn, twilight, dawn, in the city of Hurqalya, The Imaginal World.

THE BEGINNING

The *Was Not*. Then one note,
The tinkling of a bell, a tiny triangle.
The rest you know.

But I want to concentrate
On the Just-Before:
What none of us could know,

What the act of creation,
If it was an act,
Made impossible.

What happened first
Was not, strictly speaking,
Possible. Yet once

You know that,
You know that you
Can stay, or go,

No matter. And if
You go, you can go
Anywhere—that far back.

PACKING TO MOVE

I come upon a letterpress poem I set
In movable type, back when I still did that—
Fall 1977. It was a poem by my favorite professor.
That September a young woman had come down
From Walla Walla to study poetry, a graduate fellow.
Late one Friday afternoon in October, long shadows
And the Inner Quad empty, I crossed toward Building 30
And there she was, sitting awkwardly on the low curb
Just outside the archway. I paused to watch for a moment,
Utterly entranced. She did not notice me. She did not
Notice anything. Only one thing was on her mind,
It had all happened that fast. I leaned against a pillar
Outside the chapel. And when he finally came, and they
Went into his office briefly, and then off toward his sad
Little faculty condo for the divorced and the unfortunate,
Then, then it was clear. A week later I brought her roses,
An absurd gesture she instantly understood. Though technically
His student, she largely taught herself, he learned from her,
And though that year and the next those of us in the workshop
Partied together almost every weekend, already she had taken him
In hand, and by the spring his drinking stopped. We had known
It was with him a race against the clock: would the Great Book
Come together before he drank himself to death? Now
It did not matter. No one questioned the "rightness"
Of the relationship. They were saving one another.
Over twenty years, they had two daughters, grown now,
And now they share the house they found off Middlefield,
Just before all the houses there became unaffordable.
I don't like poems with lessons, but in the end
This was the one love story everyone around them
Needed to see, needed to be in a cameo way a part of,
To know that love is not by definition tragic, to know
That when it comes it comes hard, and then no rule
Can intervene to separate the one back into two,
To tear them in sanctioned violence from their future.

UNCOMPREHENDING

Packing up the poems from fall 2015—yes, *those* poems—
The thickest file by far, astounding how the drafts
And counter-drafts went back and forth, selves
Coming to mind on the unanticipated page, you somehow
The genius I had overlooked—or had you held back,
Deliberately? I will never know. The precision of your
Phrasing, the therefore-amusing moments when
For whatever reason you went off: I felt useful, then,
Simply voicing those possible corrections. We knew
By mid-September. . .And then the unbelievable poem,
The rain and the train, your scientific mind working
Its poetic logic on every possible outcome, however
Futile, disastrous, or blessed, and in the end deciding
The train was precisely what you were waiting for. This
Is why we use the word "grief" sparingly: we don't like
To admit that we don't understand, that something
Made sense and then suddenly it didn't, or worse yet,
Was simply gone—snatched away as if by a spell,
Which indeed was what happened, the witches
Coming out of the wood to make good on the secret
Promises within, behind "The Disquieting Muses."

ARRIVAL IN BURRAVOE

Though we could have simply taken the channel up to Burravoe,
We rowed past the Ulsta ferry slip, past the commercial docks,
To a simple tie-up on the north-end dock. From there,
Like any other people, we caught the old bus along the south
Of Yell, the B9081. Past the Loch of Ulsta, Coppister, Hamnavoe,
And Alba was silent, listening no doubt to the echoes of Bishop
In my own head, the Nova Scotia passengers who knew each other
From far back, the family stories, what he said, what she said,
The moose in the road that jarred them from their stories
With its feral miracle. Here the sheep roamed and the border collies
Herded, their sharp barks faint in the wind. The way everyone
Seemed to know Alba was the way I would know a child
I had grown up with if my parents had also grown up with her,
And their parents: I was taken for granted, not a stranger,
Merely a mystery. It was enough that I was there. We got off
Near the Burravoe Primary School, and walked south and up
A low rise, deep tufted grass with its spindrift green in the blue
Sheen of the low sun, and the house was stark white, with a broken
Fence and some outbuildings. Park House. "This is my house,"
She said. "Honestly, it's a wreck. You would be better there—"
She pointed across an expanse of perhaps a dozen houses
To a tidy, pretty tan duplex across from what looked like
The oldest house on the island, which it was. . ."That's the old
Haa Museum," she said. "The place just down from it.
I Marybank Road." Those are the places for people who live
In time, apart. Family stories, tragedies, what you just came from,
There in your head on the bus." "Then why am I here"—
My first trace of annoyance. She ignored me, shaking
Her black hair out into the wind. "I am going to make supper,"
She said, "Shepherd's pie, which you don't much like,
And then I am going to read to you from a prophet,
Jeanette Winterson. If you fall asleep as I read, you may stay
As long as you like." "She's not Scottish," I said. "Manchester.
London." "She knows what she knows," Alba replied.
"There is always a journey inside a journey. I will read to you
From *Sexing the Cherry*. If you fall asleep I will know
It is your story." She is unsurprised at my wonder.
"The person who introduced me to *Sexing the Cherry*
Was a miracle long ago," I said. "No," she replied.
"It was one of several me's you have encountered.

I never said that you were wise. But you live love
The way love should be lived and you deserve what you have not."
And thus I sat down at the table in the makeshift kitchen.

SHEPHERD'S PIE

2 pound potatoes, peeled and cubed

"But wait," I said, as she began the meal—"if you know
To read *Sexing the Cherry* to see if I will sleep, you must
Already know that I will." She turned.

2 tablespoons sour cream

"You are no more or less perfect than I, no more
Or less fallible," she said. "You and I share an origin.
The difference is that I have been there and you
Only think you have. Your mind has utterly cluttered
Your life. Even now you are worshipping me
As a prophetess. I only know what I know, and I
Know you, as I know the veracity of metempsychosis."

1 large egg yoke, black pepper, 1 tablespoon extra-virgin olive oil.

"So you have been me," I said. She laughed.
"No, silly," she said. "There was no need.
Besides, it was more fun not being you—
Not to play with you, as others have,
But actually to be present with you
When you do whatever it is you are going to do."

1 ¾ pounds of ground beef or lamb.

"Why aren't you using lamb?" I asked, as the scent
Crossed the room. She laughed again. "You would not
Have eaten it," she said. "You will be on the expensive side
To keep, if you stay. But there are ways."

1 chopped carrot, 1 chopped onion, 2 tablespoons butter, 2 tablespoons flour,
Worcestershire sauce to taste, ½ cup baby peas, paprika, parsley

The mix moved from the saucepan and two frying pans to the
        casserole.
She placed it under the broiler and said aloud: *"Every journey conceals*
Another journey within its lines: the path not taken and the forgotten
Angle. These I are journeys I wish to record. Not the ones I made,

But the ones I might have made, or perhaps did make in some other
Place or time." She laughed. "I was right about you, I'll give myself
That much," she said. "Time to eat." All told it had been half an
hour.

THE NARROW ROAD TO THE FAR NORTH

I can tell you that if you choose to go
It will be very difficult to return. In that sense
It is not a choice. More like birth, death—
That given. If it calls you and you fail to go,

Your life will be over. You will live a shade
Among the Dantean shades Dante himself
Knew so well. Not among them, Beatrice—
More alive to him than any living soul.

But also not a choice. That, too,
We do not control. As unlikely as it seems,
Be patient. The call will call, not once only,
But for a time. It wants you. It wants you.

It will make sure it reaches your marrow.
And if, then, you refuse, then it will relent.
You were unworthy. But you are not
Unworthy. That is its secret.

COMFORT FOR A CHILD

That fixed point in space
Toward which we each are moving,

If we are—in terms of luminosity
Or "absolute magnitude" (32.6 light-years/

10 parsecs)—we accidentally
Suggest that we will never get there

I think we are each
Fixed points in space

And the illusion is not mortality
But motion

Long ago now you said
You wanted a body next to yours
When you awaken

That may happen
Or it may not

But it does not change who we are
What we are

It does not change how the point
Fans out into a galaxy

More beautiful than the wreath
Of smoke from your cigarette

Once we are there
But till then ash

THE PASSAGE AND THE PASSAGE OF A DAY

He awoke, after a day of which he had scant memory,
To Fortunata's face, her hair as Alba's all around him
And that cloak a gentle darkness in the dawn. Still,
He started. "Shhh," she said. "Don't take your eyes
Off mine. I want to teach you how to be a point
Of light." "—What—" She smiled an uncommon,
Quiet smile. "I saw what you were thinking, yesterday,
From the boat," she said. "You have no idea how close
You are to right. But for now, here we are, with our stories
From the Memory Palace, and so for now we must practice."
"The Memory Palace," he said, I said, struggling to recall—
"That is not from *Sexing the Cherry*," I said. "It is from
Rushdie." "Of course," she said. "Stay still. Did you really
Think each novelist tells a different story, each poem
Is different? We are all trying to get back to somewhere
We already are." She placed her hands on either side
Of my head. "Follow my eyes," she said. Of course
At first, as always, I sank in—her eyes were
Obsidian, depthless, where one would want to go
And never leave. Then the sensation of a sudden
Lift, as of being swept up in a fierce soft wind,
And depths of darkness turned to light—distant at first,
But then not nearer—rather, encompassing, different
Magnitudes and luminosities, all the colors with their
Various gravities, with the spiral trail, like that wreath
From a cigarette, and I at the center—but I was not I,
And she, there as well, was not apart from whoever it was
Who was seeing. And all fixed in space—no motion,
Or not any we would measure with our common tools.
Something. "Hmmm," she said: at that moment
Her eyes returned to obsidian, that compensatory
Vision. "So you can do it," she said. "You are. You are
Jordan." "And you are Kara Köz." "Yes," she said.
"The distances are fixed. I thought—" But then he knew.

LUMINOSITY AND MAGNITUDE

The trip back to the Ulsta commercial docks was quick,
With the wind behind them and the following sea, the tide
Coming in. No one said a thing. As for me, I was running
Jordan's story through my mind, over and over, his reincarnations
Like an endless loop of a kind to frighten Tibetans. Dog-Woman
Had warned me of this several times, from youth on, before she too
Was born anew, and anew, more distant with each re-birth.
Alba was standing on the bow, letting the spray fall
Over her yellow Avanti weather jacket and salopettes,
Her stance wide, oblivious and thrilled as far as I could tell.
At the dock she tied the bow expertly as I drew in the stern—
Either a fast learner or someone secretly having done this
Many times. We thanked the kind fisherman and went to wait
For the old bus to Burravoe. "I think," she said, "You are confusing
Luminosity and magnitude. I know where you have been, how many
Times your heart broke on this trip home. But posit that artificial
Point, ten parsecs: there your magnitude and luminosity remain
Unchanged. It's just that here no one can see your magnitude.
You appear an ordinary, somewhat desperate failure. But
Luminosity—that is what we choose to shift when we accept
The fiction of our motion from the Imaginal to the phenomenal.
Your energy here is minor and sad. The radiation you give off
Is as confused and as discouraged as it is attractive. It is the source
Of most confusion in this world." "I am tired of lessons," I said.
"Kara Köz—" she replied. I turned back from the end of the dock.
"The secret that, once revealed to Akbar, destroyed Sikri,
And the Mogor dell'Amore vanished by morning. The answer:
It was not simply Khan and Köz. Remember? There was
A child." Impossible to summarize the eons that passed
Between us just then. I said: *"The Enchantress of Florence*
Is crucially unclear just there, five pages from the end."
"It could not be clearer," Alba replied. Eye-to-eye:
"Why," I asked, "Would you even consider bringing a child
Into this world, knowing what you know, what we have seen?"
"Because," she said in perfect measure, "We have seen it."

JUST THEN

Just then   in the night beside her

        That one tiny sound   pitch-perfect

Across space   it had no business crossing

        And the eccentric point of light   that same

Magnitude

Yet suddenly intensely luminous   then quiet

        Together they made   the words   vanish

                All of them

So that in the morning   before Alba woke

        I wrote   this translation

Which is what you are reading   these terrible ordeals

        Are real   in the context we have chosen

But what was true   before the beginning   of this universe

        Remains true   We are wholly other

The Kiowa were more than right   We do not simply

        Have kin in the night sky

                We are the kin   in the night sky

PARK HOUSE, BURRAVOE, YELL, ZE2 9AY

Park House stood near the top of a long hill overlooking
Much of the rest of Burravoe, and a small, picturesque bay.
For those conversant in Anglo-American poetry it had a great deal
In common with Plath and Hughes' Court Green in Devon—
Old, one of the first houses in Burravoe, of stone and felt,
An impermanent roof at best, though the house itself
Whitewashed and luminous all around, as Alba would have
Demanded. But unlike Court Green it needed
A great deal of work, which I wondered if Alba had also
Intended, as it was in its way useful. Though the kitchen
Had decent fittings and a tile floor, the plumbing throughout
Was cracked and leaking, and the roof had leaked through,
Destroying wallpaper and walls, some studs rotten,
Electrical wires loose along the ceiling and all
The interior stonework needing repointing—it amused me
To experiment just enough to discover you could make
The chimney collapse by pulling just one stone
From the masonry. And the dreadful red carpet
On the staircase. Again, always the question:
Why bother, if you can leave at any time? But Alba,
Knowing the immeasurable magic of leaving,
Came here precisely because of the intrinsically different
Nature of human connection—its volatility, its sentimentality,
Its resistance to theory, its passion, its Julia Kristeva dare in
In the Beginning Was Love. For money we had to live quite
Frugally on my retirement, though Alba had her way
Of making money last. New roof felt, which alone
Would start to leak again in a few years, though
Under asphalt shingles would survive for 20?
Slate? We made our lists, took the ferry to Toft
And hired a van for the drive to Lerwick.
Hay & Co. for the plumbing, Jewson for electrical,
For studs, for lath and plaster, the living room
Flooring, and the matter of the roof—slate would dignify both
history and the island, but only asphalt shingles
Fit the budget. . .Alba shrugged. Slate. Slate meant
No felt, which would disintegrate decades before the slate
Began to crack, but laying slate took patience. No rush,
We agreed without a word, as Alba handed me a single,

Rough-hewn slate. We worked well together,
Alba and I. We were rebuilding a home.

DEATH SPIRAL

Of course   at a certain point   there seems no way   out
     without power

The left wing stalled
     And the plane pivoting left

As the right wing   paradoxically provides
     All the lift   needed for the crash

Power in a plane   comes from the engine
     In life   it depends—

How not to think of Plath   in her holding pattern
     Ariel done   but unseen

The Bell Jar out   under a pseudonym
     Just a novel   among novels

And that terrible weather
     You can feel   that loss of airspeed

You can feel that left wing   drop
     If you are clever   and have the altitude

You can pull out   of a death spiral   without power
     But you have   to want to

Plath had a kind of makeshift
     Crash crew   in place

But there is also a luxury   in the drop
     Its certainty   the giddiness of the spiral

Almost as if one were once again
     A child on a carousel

The long-lost maternal comfort   finally present
     Only in the moment   the eyes finally close

LESSONS AND PRAYERS

And thus they were walking in the cool of their day,
Which was always and everywhere, until they chose otherwise.
Finally the central question coalesced, and I said—
But Alba answered: "Galaxies apart, we manifest
Our parallels—yearnings—through gravitational similarities:
Stars with exoplanets much like this one, centrifugal force
Just outstripping the centripetal of the black hole at the center,
Through which it all begins again in a way I cannot describe.
It will. Think how many times before you must have done this,
With your particular yearning, the speed of your expansion—
Thus this place, this planet, where Edwin Hubble first proposed
Expansion of the universe, $v=H_oD$, with "D" the "proper distance"
From our planet to any galaxy and "v" the derivative velocity
With "H_o," "Hubble's constant," 71 kilometers per second for every
Megaparsec in distance. . .In short, your motion, given your apparent
Fixity, caught my attention. Of course you return here, over and over:
Weary of stasis and motion, you sought love. Without mathematics,
The earthly theories of reincarnation wither into sadness. . .
Love is what gives you freedom to go or stay. That is the reason why
This time, if you so choose, should be your last, or if not,
Why you can go and come at will."

"And the child?"

"Our children here are stars," she replied. "When she arrives,
She will arrive for the same reason you arrived, except that,
Knowing what you know, you will liberate her from the curse
Under which you have laboured for so long you think
          that it is yours."

FORTUNATA KÖZ

Three months passed. We repaired the roof and furnace, added insulation under the eaves, and the house became warm. We armed the stairs with Berber, and I laid the *de rigueur* laminate hardwood floor in the living room; new circuit breakers, wiring, plumbing, the rotted studs replaced and the lathe and plaster done: she was well on her way to homeship. Alba, for her part, was as thrilled as I have seen with her supple roundness; her miracle, among those several, was her joy in human mutability, at the end rejected in Spenser's *Mutabilitie Cantos*. And then, of course, she understood what few do, creating a being who will cross uncrossable boundaries—"Because we have seen it." Still, there was a moment then—"What are the most important pages of *Sexing the Cherry?*" she asked me one day when I'd come in with groceries from Toft. "That's easy," I said. "The nonfiction essay on the nature of time and space smack in the middle of the book, pp. 99-101." We liked quoting page numbers at one another. Sometimes an entire conversation would consist of nothing but page numbers from different, unnamed books. "No, of course you'd be wrong, silly," she replied. "It's the part about grafting, pp. 84-85. Where Jordan tries to explain to his mother that *the tree would still be female although it had not been born from seed, but she said such things had no gender and were a confusion to themselves. . .But the cherry grew, and we have sexed it, and it is female.*" "Hmm. . ." I said, "which is another way of saying 'You chose me. You chose this.'" "I just wanted to see if you were paying attention," she said. "Men get dreamy when women are pregnant." "Do they," I said. "You dream about being a woman in the next life," she said. "No doubt you will. What we become out there"—she pointed toward the sky—"affects our luminosity here, including our gender. It will be interesting, coming around to find you, those next times we inaugurate return."

And it came to pass that the days were accomplished that she should be delivered, and she bore a daughter, whom we named after her other true first name, "Fortunata," and after her mother's true last name, "Köz." It was then that Alba saw the orb and heard the sound and returned to her place in the galaxy we name with letters and numbers, Gleise 667 Cc, and it was left to me to raise Fortunata there on the island of Yell, where I had much-needed help in Burravoe and walked her countless mornings down the hill to the primary school, and everyone admired her precocity and long, jet-black hair until, at about the age of ten, she came into my bed one night with a story of an orb

65

in the sky and a sound like one from a perfect tuning fork, and I knew then it was time to take her to her own place there, to meet her mother and to dance in the impossibly still distance of our shared galaxy. When she and I returned, she would begin her own, unhurried search for the someone who would know—as she could tell on first sight—the luminosity and magnitude of home.

THE LAST POEM

I know. . .But I cannot apologize. *In medias res*
We expect at the beginning of stories, not at the end.

There is so much that you want to know. . .But remember
How this all began, with something as simple and sentimental

As a house removal ("home move" in American English)
And how far we have come, how in your reading here

You have witnessed events beyond any that words should be able
To tell, and yet here they are: you can go over them, and over,

And they will become more remarkable, not less. I don't need
To promise, and my vanity is ordinary. I know. You wonder:

Yes, I am unspeakably grateful to have witnessed this, and to know
Where I belong, where I will go and with whom. If any of you

Sees that orb in the sky, like no other, and at the same time
Hears the sound that should never cross space, you too will know

It is time to go, time for mutability that makes death look
Like a sham magician's trick. But if you never see the orb

Or hear the sound, you should at least accept this comfort—yes,
It all is real, what you have read here in this universal night.

STREET RACING

FIRST SUNDAY OF ADVENT, 1967

Today it's nearly dusk
When the snow gathers, finally,
On the lawn, the tired side

Of the wind turned white
And settling down.
I watch the steady storm

From my mother's rocking chair
Upstairs, all room lights off.
The house below is quiet.

My father, too, may be staring
Out the window, straining to see
The fender of the Chevrolet

He banged up on a tree this afternoon;
He will not speak for hours, or days.
My mother, having trouble reading

In the intricate silence,
Lays down her book and glides into the kitchen:
She adds potatoes to the sizzling roast.

Up here it scarcely matters what they do.
Through the lulling constancy of snow,
I hear the muffled grunts and spatters

Of their need, and still I sit,
A dream apart from love. For who am I
To cry, entranced with the night,

And lost to them as if,
Unseeing, I looked down
From the darkness of heaven?

TO THE POET

Long Garden,
Cliveden, England

These words
Are the perfect solitude
One step from where you are.
I move behind them, a shadow
Eluding the quickest eye,
Passing like a presence
Unidentified across a hedgewall
On some summer afternoon.
What holds you is the wondering,
A kind of knowing how you are alive.
The step you take
Will find me moving too,
In woods surrounding you, where you have seen
A fieldmouse darting under leaves
To find its secret trails,
Where I have been. You hardly know
How near you come to me.

THE HOUSE WHERE NIGHT FELL

A long time I crowded the fireplace,
My brother and sister close by, the loud fire
Of our play reduced to ashes, the day greying:
Lost in the flame, in the twittering log, I heard
The last cries of the wood finch, of the mourning dove
Nesting in the pine by the window. Calling back
The day, they sang unseen as the grey shade
Came silently over the snow, into the yard,
Turning it ragged and cold, turning the tree old,
Giving the cries a chill—and the log burned
Bright as a tropical bird, warbling flame,
The great pine log from an old tree, dark as the night.

THE COMPANION

Before I turned to you
It had arrived, companion of the moonlight
Resting on your troubled face.

Asleep, you could not discern
The way that it slipped in,
Without sound, between the window

And the window frame;
A mere sense
Of solitary movement against

The rising storm,
As sheep on a coastal hill
Turn one by one from the gale.

More gentle than my touch
It washed over you, made you stir,
Brought you in from the wind.

EMBERS

Restless at dusk they slowly return
From the pasture, their wake a thin tangle of grass,
Their lowing the embers of night
As they move with a will to one place.
When darkness, thick as ash, rides in
On the tide of the nearby sea, they move
Slightly in sleep, and illumine the barn
In the wake of their murmuring light.

FIREWATCHERS

Sunset Beach, California

You are the latent fullness
Of an unsteady wind, so when you dance
In the middle of their tight ring,
Let their faces feel all that you contain;
Let them, in each other's gaze, see how
Their faces become you, flickering
In your illumined breeze.

For around them is your medium,
Endless and turbulent as the blue
Froth perpetually cresting
Night's invisible sea. But now
You must show them the flame
Potent in these gusts,
Claiming the spontaneous power of quick air.

COLLECTS

They would fit in my hand, all these stones,
So slightly they rest in the brown stubble grass;
I stare at them, thinking of great ladies' eyes;
As silent as secrets from heaven, they watch.

They are scattered and beautiful—how shall I gather them?
I touch one, I find two beside it.
I shall gather them wordlessly, glancing and turning,
Grasping them just as they turn back to stone.

GUTTER, FILLED WITH RAIN

Night
Spills over its sides.
Light-years
Rest at your feet.
Scattered in the slightest breeze,
Distant
Almost beyond measure,
The star beside you
Waits
For the calm air,
Its perfect presence
Hovering
Beneath the passing nearness
Of water.

IMPACT

The work of wings

was always freedom, fastening
one heart to every falling thing.
                                    —Li-Young Lee

The freedom to fall:
Was it so bad, gliding then

At altitude, the flight
Of the child? Raised in turbulence,

One too often erases
Part of the picture,

The bruises, the tears:
From here, five decades out,

It almost looks like a straight
Line, smooth and unencumbered.

The stars turned; the moon
Alternated as it does with the sun,

That unparalleled blueness all around.
Spiraling, wounded in the most ordinary

Of accidents, yet absolutely distinct,
The bullet in the heart, I feel my wings

Contract, and my body, luminous, grows
Heavy with the gravity of the land

Rising to meet me, its beloved and lost
People and the last word, someone calling my name.

MY FATHER

I want to remember something
That never occurred: I
And my father are one.

We walk as one down a sunny
Street in Avalon, so close we don't
Know we are two: releasing each other

From the despair that will span decades,
We puzzle over an intricate problem in aerodynamics,
Parasitic drag, or the set of piston rings

To be replaced in the old Plymouth—
Careful work that contents us. The perfect
Storm of failed love, not once only,

Like all those hurricanes we barely
Weathered, or won't, cannot
Touch us. Unknowing, we keep ourselves

Company, not realizing that this
Is the source and center of our happiness,
This illusion that lifts like a wing before vanishing.

NEED

Loneliness was an elixir
After the crowds and shop stalls
And Romans, the Occupied by turn
Contentious and hopeful, and everyone,
Everyone needing something, always.

Need cannot be satisfied,
Can never be satisfied:
Need for: for healing,
For release from demons, for
Life restored—is merely,

In the end, a yearning
To be the one one knows one is not.
Despite the gossip and rumours,
Jesus yearned to be who
He was. He did not

Need the isolation of the mountains
To know how deep a single
Particle of self could be, how
At any moment it could open out
Into the companionable universe.

Yet he chose the mountains,
Their labyrinthine Judean aridity,
As he also chose Mary.
And there was a tremor
In the innermost heart of God.

Impossible, such a thing.
But Mary touched him. They
Touched, kissed. And when, then,
He was not alone, he became that man
Who came late to need.

STREET RACING

For J.B.

The lines have been torn to shreds under your feet.
You can make a list for comfort—it won't work:
Yellow and white lines, luminous in the dark
To keep the chaos of acceleration from defeat
Become the savage colors of your heart
That sees the way to go and one fierce speed
Drawn out from him, but more from your own need
To outrun everything you stopped but couldn't start.

Did he do this—can you blame him?—or, insatiate,
Were both of you street racing as you said
You never would on all the backroads of the coastal range,
The lines peeling away beneath the rubber heat
No pigment could withstand, no daub, color, word
Or even memory? No—no line remains to mark the change.

HEALING

The days are full of sleep. Waking,
One sees the keep of the new white fields, staking

A claim to what before were sidewalks, yards
And streets. Blurring the familiar wards

Or seems to ward away the daily changes time requires,
The work of dying; living by one's own desires,

Or dreams, or both, one moves past places once familiar,
Now returned to strangeness by the time of year,

The time of snow. And this is good, to move as if asleep,
When waking is bitter cold, and cold runs deep,

Almost far down enough to touch that feeling
We cannot quite name—not hope—a kind of healing

Of all that time requires, though time runs deep
And seems to, does not, threaten us in sleep.

PORTIONING THE SOUL

Near Hartsel, Colorado

Some days nothing can be done.
Yet, driving, coming over
Wilkerson Pass into a valley
Thirty miles wide, twenty miles long,
You see how survival
Might be possible:

You portion out your soul.
Over there, in that stand of piñon pine
Ten miles away, is part of you you love,
A part that is not ashamed:
You place it there, deliberately,
So that, months later or years,

Still you know where to find it—
Or that other part of you,
As trusting as a child, that goes
Into the palomino at the far edge
Of the ranch on Highway Nine,
So that you know, though one day

She will die, she will run and run
And be both tame and wild,
Among her kin, shivering in the cold
Or magnificent in the sun,
Growing into everything that part of you
Believed in, even if she must fade

And fail, even if she must. Perhaps
Her foals will cherish it unknowing.
But always you will know
Where this time took place,
The time you portioned out your soul
For safekeeping so that, finally, it would be safe.

NORTH OF LAST CHANCE

Highway 71, Colorado

We have come so far,
It is over. Now to know,
For certain. . .Yet each
Emerging grain of next fall's
Hay gleams in the sun, each now
Inflected with this reality.

How you know it was real:
The land follows you, each furrow
Running behind, falling farther back
With each mile, yet stubbornly
Refusing to be one thing, to smooth out.
How many things you were, how many things.

GEMINI

Inconceivably foolish, to have bought
A house because of the luminous
Plastic stars on the bedroom ceilings.
Even to have come back
A second time, at night,
To be assured—as daylight
Through huge windows seemed to say
Come, so the plastic stars on that
February night, arranged in pretend
Constellations, burst through the darkness,
Seemed to say, *Home, this is your*
Home. If I could have known
The sorrow that would arise—could I
Have prevented it, somehow? The stars
Are still here, watching over my nights
Alone, as if to say, *You are ours,*
Now, you are one of us, almost.

LAST WEDNESDAY IN MARCH

March 28, 2007

At the end comes an abridgment,
The conclusion of unnecessary speech,
An agreement between the spoken

And the spoken to. The light is sharp,
Raw, a winter light made spring
By spring's incessant coming.

It has nothing to do with us.
Yet, waiting within it, finally
Released to sufficience, the year's

Terrors and fears dropping away,
We reach an equivalence, our lives
For the light, and for the light, silence.

THE WOUND AND THE CURE OF WORDS

One day you may fade into irrelevance,
And I, by then, absolved of alcohol
Or drinking less, will look clear-eyed
Upon this ordinary house, and place,

And go to work because it is
My work, and return home to companionable
Loneliness or, should grace intervene,
A lover, gentle and serene.

You would be sometimes a memory,
Sometimes less, and in my happiness
I would feel you only on some days
The wound that you will ever be.

HOMEBUILT

For Michael Ramsey-Perez,
Menlo Park, California, 1978

Such bangings and hammerings one floor down,
In that garage apartment, as we cooked too much
Spaghetti, drank, and sang to Willie Nelson,
Jerry Jeff Walker, Emmylou Harris—such
Sheet metal your landlord riveted, and so late,
His own homebuilt to lift him to the *kyrie eleison*
Of the sky. Close to the earth, we wrote poems; at dawn,
While I slept, you burned them. Nothing was good enough

To keep except our lives, those nights, the wing
Below finally taking shape as we peered through,
Laid aside in the end for the fuselage, that crucial
Home that might have held us. Rising now, as you sing
Because you must, the flawed song of all that you are due,
Remember, as I do, what burned and flew from our kind
          crucible.

THE NIGHT OF THE HURRICANE

At first it was just a storm.
Then, louder and louder as night fell,
It seemed a whirlwind out of the cloud
To bring the whole house into being,
Though not benevolent: the studs and joists
Groaned, shivering, and the rooms
Seemed to grow in increments, as if
Severed from the frame beneath them,
As if the foundations were a bed
For lying-in. Rigid in my top bunk,
I could see the ceiling plywood
Flex, hear the nails letting go,
A shingle rising up and away
And more, and more. At three A.M.,
When the siding of the neighbor's house
Blew clean away, my father piled us
Into our 1966 Chevelle, and we went
Looking in that blizzard without snow
For the last way out, the 21st Street bridge,
Perhaps still there. One railing came
Into view, not two. Then salt water,
Seeping from the channel through the doors.
My father made a choice, gunned the engine.
I didn't think to ask him if he knew
Or if, like me, he had simply had enough.

RAIN

Unfaithful, reason fades,
And you are here
As on the day we met,
When all that reason knew

Was your quiet voice,
Eyes of astonishment.
No: a thousand rationales
Left us, in the end, alone.

In memory, once reason left
Its keys upon the table,
You are here, as you were,
Shaking the rain from your hair.

SNOW

How should I speak to you of snow,
I who have so long lived in its presence?
Snow, and the winter night that seems
Endless, though time passes and the day

Imperceptibly grows? I am at home
Where light grows from the ground
And darkness falls from the sky,
The remnant of the tribe of Eden.

In Jerusalem, yesterday, eight inches
Of snow fell from nowhere, it seemed,
And the Hassids covered themselves
With umbrellas, and laughed. And in

Ramallah, where the streets were paved
Treacherously in white, one member
Of the Palestinian Security Forces
Threw a snowball at another, who ran,

Laughing, his AK-47 hugged close to his chest
Like a toy, and in Hebron, a little girl
Sat beside a window, wearing knitted mittens
And a cap. Too late to pretend the world

Sometimes visits beneficence on the most wounded
Or wounding, I remember their illumined faces,
Their televised occasion of joy, or self-forgetfulness,
Or simply self, that old bright self from which

I would speak to you unsentimentally
From this place where selves are best,
Or best-loved, when most ordinary, where
Light rises only when darkness falls.

EXIT WOUND

What is the pulse that lives
In the stone of the *souk,*
Atextual, not Biblical, inscribed
In crevices where no prayer resides,
Those tiny folded notes like sparrows
Fluttering over the canvas roots
Or whitewashed domes of the vendors,
Alert to the tiniest movement, the something
Where a prayer could have been—
Or upwelling from Tel Dan, or just north,
Water over the cedar roots, the brilliant grass
And rifles aimed, Lebanon, or rockets
From above, among the tittering birds
And laundry hanging from close balconies,
The rotting food and excrement and
This is the daily balance, not a jot
Or tittle more than what will, at any moment,
Leave an exit wound of which this is one.

ACKNOWLEDGMENTS

Over the past 31 years, this work would not have been possible without the remarkable mothers of my six children—Nate, Georgia, Thomas, Hart, Peter, and Faye—and thus here I would like deeply to thank Lesley Wright, Laura Rigal, Rachel Sauter, Laura Crossett, and Elizabeth Wisnosky.

I also wish to thank the publications in which some of these poems previously appeared: *Now*, Saint Julian Press; the *Atlantic;* the *New Republic;* the *Southern Review;* the *Threepenny Review; Occident; Prairie Schooner;* the *Christian Science Monitor;* and *The Uncommon Touch: Fiction and Poetry from the Stanford Writing Workshop,* ed. John L'Heureux (Stanford, CA: Stanford Alumni Association, 1989).

Ron Starbuck, the publisher and CEO of Saint Julian Press, Houston, has been an exceptionally patient and able editor and friend throughout this process. My debt to him remains profound.

ABOUT THE AUTHOR

Thomas Simmons taught for 24 years in the Department of English at the University of Iowa; in the spring of 2016 he started something new and has been writing ever since. Before that, he was an assistant and associate professor in the Program in Writing and Humanistic Studies at the Massachusetts Institute of Technology; before that, he was a doctoral student in English at the University of California, Berkeley, a Wallace Stegner Fellow in Creative Writing at Stanford, and a Stanford University undergraduate. His seven previous books, one of which (*The Unseen Shore: Memories of a Christian Science Childhood*, Beacon Press, 1991) caused some offense in Boston, may be viewed at amazon.com site listed below. He lives in Grinnell, Iowa.

Visit his Amazon author page at: *amazon.com/author/Thomas Simmons.*

TYPEFACE: Perpetua Titling MT

The half title and title pages are set in the typeface Perpetua Titling MT for the book's title. Perpetua is a serif typeface designed by English sculptor and stonemason Eric Gill for the British Monotype Corporation at around 1925, when Gill's reputation as a leading artist-craftsman was high.

TYPEFACE: GARAMOND – Garamond

The poems in this book are set in the typeface Garamond, named for the sixteenth-century Parisian engraver Claude Garamont. The font was originally designed in 1530 by printer Robert Estienne.